Midflight

Midflight

David Corcoran

Four Way Books

Tribeca

Library of Congress Cataloging-in-Publication Data

Names: Corcoran, David, 1947-2019, author.
Title: Midflight / David Corcoran.
Description: New York : Four Way Books, 2022.
Identifiers: LCCN 2021046451 | ISBN 9781954245105 (trade paperback) |
ISBN 9781954245181 (epub)
Subjects: LCGFT: Poetry.
Classification: LCC PS3603.O734147 M53 2022 | DDC 811/.6--dc23
LC record available at https://lccn.loc.gov/2021046451

This book is manufactured in the United States of America and printed on
acid-free paper.

Four Way Books is a not-for-profit literary press. We are grateful for the assistance
we receive from individual donors, public arts agencies, and private foundations
including the NEA, NEA Cares, Literary Arts Emergency Fund, and the
New York State Council on the Arts, a state agency.

We are a proud member of the Community of Literary Magazines and Presses.

Contents

Foreword

The poems of David Corcoran are as haunting as they are haunted. The settings seem familiar enough at first, whether bucolic or prosaic: a woodland trail littered with last year's leaves, a dirt-floor basement, a parking lot beside an abandoned world's fair. But the scene can quickly turn disquieting or go akilter, even as the poet savors its strangeness or appraises his own bewilderment. Acquaintances enter and exit, but some are deceased. Automobiles may gently tumble down long staircases. Summer and winter can coexist in Escher-like fashion. The giddiest of moments may pivot and reveal itself as deeply troubling.

The reason for all of this is logical: David Corcoran's poems are based not only on his life but frequently on his dreams. And some of his creations—as with instrumental compositions that allude to works of prose—could be deemed "tone poems," galvanized by a painting, a magazine cover or even a century-old comic strip.

I once asked David if a certain poem was inspired by a real experience, and his revelatory answer was, "Yes, it was based on a dream." He paints still lifes of reveries and nightmares the way Georgia O'Keeffe captures the spirits of plants and flowers. The effect is that of an impressionist artist's interpretation of a surrealist vision: Claude Monet rendering a Salvador Dalí landscape.

David Corcoran was valedictorian of the Nyack High School class that I attended, and we renewed our friendship twenty years later when he was writing for *The New York Times* and I was writing for the stage. As the respected and revered editor of its *Science Times* section, David consistently helped his brilliant contributors to be their most compelling. But in the last decades of his life, he focused his transformative gifts upon his poetry. And while this gracious and very funny man never took himself too seriously, he pursued the honing of his craft studiously, humbly, and passionately under the mentorship of such luminaries as Martha Rhodes, Patricia Carlin, Henri Cole, Alan Shapiro and Marie Ponsot.

He took to shyly sharing his newest works with me, including this breathtaking collection which moved and stunned me, one impeccably crafted poem after the next. As a musician, I deeply admire his cadences and pauses, and the ineffable lilt of his voice, with not a word wasted but each selected and perfectly placed upon the page. For me, it feels as if the cryptic "lines" of Stephen Crane have been joined by the symbiosis with nature found in haiku, then lavished with David's wit, humanity and yearning.

The course and tone of David's life and work were shaped by a tragic childhood event. Before his second birthday, shortly before the birth of his brother John, while he and his mother Ruth were visiting relatives in the Midwest, David's father, a successful photographer and journalist for *Science Illustrated*, was killed in a dreadful automobile accident near the family's hometown of Nyack, New York. The crash, and unanswered questions regarding that terrible night, imbued David's life with the longing for "what might have been." (The cover image of this collection comes from David's desk; the 1941 Dodge is very likely the same make as the one that landed on John Corcoran's body after he'd been thrown from its driver's seat. Note the somber notation David made of the car's weight, as if its impact could ever be measured in numbers.)

You will find the father whom David barely knew quietly drifting into a poem every now and then, like an apologetic night watchman making his midnight rounds, regretting his intrusion. In the stunning conclusion to this volume, David unflinchingly recreates the horrific accident that altered the course of his life and that of his family, doing so with a lyricism that soars despite the gravity of its outcome.

In the poem "Physical," David recreates with the sparest of brushstrokes an examination given him by his grandfather, a doctor. The poet places his late father in the scene, dressed in his Army uniform, who *"looks away, aware somehow / of what will happen. He knows / I'll never know him."* After reading that, I said to David that if his grandfather's stethoscope had been sensitive enough, he would have heard the sound of heartbreak.

Here, graced by his wit, his poignant bliss in life, and his loving surrender to its inherent sadness, are some of the finest poems by one of the finest human beings one could ever know.

—Rupert Holmes

Rupert Holmes is a Tony® and Edgar Award-winning lyricist, author and composer.

The Lake

They've left you by the water
to wait
till they call your name—

Sun, high in the sky,
pulls lower, lengthens the swimmers

Trees hold the light,
breathe it out luxuriantly

———

each finger swollen & prunish
yet you go back
under

the bottom is soft silt
riverteeth
test your soft feet, foam

rises in still water
clotted with growth

———

the sky darkens,
wind builds, and rain's
first shoots spatter
the late bathers

a gash of lightning & you head
for cover

———————

after: the lake a broth of
bones scales & sand, cupped lilies
& complicated weeds
that catch your legs
in their twiny arms

———————

the taste like iron,
far back in your throat

you could sink & live at the bottom
open your eyes
water cool, the shore

alight with small fires.

Alone

For Johnny

I call your name, call louder.
Call and call. The cries still
pierce me. The street's
a stretch of gray water, houses
either bank and cars drift by,
solid and silent though a woman
at a window asks *Are you lost?*
And so plainly I am.

Timothy

About the brother you never knew,
The one named Timothy, who
Died: Your parents didn't tell you how.
You'll never know. You didn't ask,
And now they're dead, so that is that.

Or maybe Timothy is just a name
They meant for you! You ever think
Of that? That he was never born
At all. Or that he was—born damaged,
Put away somewhere. And now,
With drugs and such, he's sort of cured,
Lives in a group home, walks around,

And rides the bus, and sprawls beside
You. Has your face. He is that man.

Night of the Opossum

I wake to crashing and a clamor of voices.
"Opossum," my father calls over his shoulder.
My mother holds a broom. The creature

scuttles from them, flattens under a sofa.
Its sickening hairless tail protrudes
and flickers like a whip. A thrust of the broom

and Mom has wounded it—slither of black
blood, hissing beneath the couch.
Now my father slides a board under the thing.

It writhes in its own blood. Gently, gently,
he slips a wicker basket over it, nods to me—
and holding this strange assemblage at each end,

we step into the dark. The night is cold
and moonless. We release him in the yard.
By the thin light from the house we see him grope

and spasm toward the bushes. In a window
my mother watches, silhouetted, still.

Physical

At the edge of Lake Michigan, moon rising—
I sit in a straight-back chair.
                              My grandfather
approaches with his worn black doctor's bag,
withdraws

a little hard-rubber tomahawk,
and strikes the soft spot just below my knee.

A thrill of reflex as my lower leg
moves of its own accord.
                              He grips
my bare shoulder,
presses his stethoscope to me. I hear

my heart beat softly. The surf pounds
and pounds. My father,

in his Army uniform,
looks away, aware somehow

of what will happen. He knows
I'll never know him.

Midway

Behind our house was a hill.
The hill led to the river.
Through layers of tightly woven brambles,
my father with a whiplike scythe
had hacked a narrow path. Red clay

and sandstone pebbles, flat red stone steps
where the hill was too steep even for boys. A boy
could get lost there, midway
                              between the house—
its orderly furniture, clean white curtains,
fiercely mitered wooden staircase—
midway between the house
and the river, silent gray expanse,
scent of decay.

                    The scythe
is long gone, left at the curb
with a thousand other rusted things
the month my father died. The house is sold, the path is gone,
landscaped out of existence. But in my own house
there's a watercolor of the old place. The painter
stands on the path, looking away
                              from the river, up the hill.

It's midsummer. Heat shimmers from every leaf.
The house looms out of the brambles,
a sandstone ship bound for open water.
The boy stands on the path, the river at his back,
staring at the house, still lost—midway.

Civilization

Side streets—a van, its side blown in—
wreckage a white sky a bathtub
dangles & every building

scabbed & burned
& gaping—but there's civilization, there's
my car on that low hill.
Keys fit, battery's dead, my family

—my mother,
dead sibs, their sons—pile in

we slide from the curb
downhill, foot off the clutch, she trembles to life—

We're in the thick traffic, my mother in front.
Push, she commands over
the hubbub, muddle,

ancient family music. Push! She cries, like a childbirth coach.
Push. Push.

Puffball

In our barn,
in a dirt-floor basement
of broken chairs, bent pitchforks,
half-bags of manure last used
in the '20s, a puffball forms
and grows.

Each humid morning I find it
taut, smooth, softly veined—
the night of my birthday, it explodes.

Yellow, deflated, flattened
like a torn glove where once
an egg, a curled dove, a perfect volleyball.
Now in the dank room,
my puffball exhales its black ashy spores.

A Visit From My Brother

He comes to me at night
as I almost fall

almost grasp
his living hand

remember how I left him
face up on a table

in the library of ashes—
in a room that echoes with light

he speaks without
hesitation: he

could always find his heart

When You Die They'll Autopsy Your Brain

In one quadrant: whiskers, insect husks,
syringes, wet ashes. In the second:
an illuminated alphabet—Apollo,
Bathysphere, Chaos, &c. The third,
your parents, shrunken & mummified,
hair & fingers eerily lifelike. And finally
a newborn, radiant as alabaster,
fragile as eggshell, who you are.

Little Nemo in Slumberland

After Winsor McCay (1869-1934)

They are looking for us! We must get down from here!
And so we do, I in my white pajamas, you

in your loincloth, your Zulu paint,
your great frightened eyes.

We clamber down the walls of blank-eyed skyscrapers
into streets teeming even at this hour.

We are ten stories tall.
A quizzical moon eyes us, peering

over half glasses. We tiptoe down a broad cross-street,
and here beneath us are steamers, docked at long green piers.

The river shimmers in the moonlight. We enter,
tide tugging at our ankles. Wide-eyed,

you utter something in your language.
I can't make it out, and you

say it louder, eyes fixed on the dark city, its empty towers,
and in the final panel, as always, I awaken, groggy—

18

my mother clutches me. *I called and called*, she says,
and I reply, *I didn't hear you!*

Anthony

At six weeks our son is already talking, saying
words—*timepiece, melon, liquor bottle*—
enunciating precisely & looking bored. His mother

is absent, leaving me to watch & bathe
& change him. And change
he does, moving bed & bedside

to the skyblue attic of this terrible empty house we thought we'd fill
when we conceived him. She paddles
in the calm surf, eyes hidden by huge black shades.

Where's Anthony
she asks, leaving off the question mark. Meaning
Your problem

I find him in his high chair
deeply focused on a cocktail shaker. His beautiful face
knitted with exasperation.

Where'd you put the Angostura bitters
he demands. I think *Who is this child*
But I know the answer.
Mine. My son, my mistake, all mine.

The Stepparents' Book

I'll watch him in his book, watching me—losing his balance, falling. I'll watch him from a hot-air balloon, rising slowly over a blank arroyo, a gravelly streambed, a granite palisade, into the cold sky. He'll watch me reading. He'll see my eyes. He'll lie on his back, his legs like sacks of sand. Once I watched him in his book of songs. He held an ax, lightly, swung it through a forest of tall conifers. Now I watch her in her book of stories, the little house so quiet she can write and write. And drink, they all do in this kingdom, fields long and yellow with hops. The sun hangs low for hours. The parents and their children play backgammon and cribbage. The rivers clear and full of stones. They'll tell stories: blood in the woods, machines that thresh and topple.

People You Knew Before You Were Born

The brother with feral eyes
the mother with hidden ones

the father, with his lost sons
the war diarist, clipping the dead

Dr. Alzheimer, with his tight smile
the father, with his lost sons

the inventor of bad news
the diarist, sighing

the doctor, slicing a bruise
the mother, with her hidden sons.

Trylon & Perisphere

The Mets lose horribly, and as I trudge to my distant car
through Flushing Meadows, a damp dismal breeze

stirs the ashes on the footpaths, kids race on skateboards
in a halide midnight blaze, dark masses of ivy

climb the '64 Pavilion's rusted towers, vast flat abandoned disks
loom overhead, bronze light leaks from the museum,

and in some corner of time, thunder growls, rain pelts the icons of an earlier Fair
as my mother and father, Ruth and John,

in their new and joyful summer before the war seized Europe, grab hands
and dash for shelter, past the bright fountains,

the many flags, the mute and patient monument that guards the time capsule—
gift to some baffled generation five thousand years away.

Somnia

life was different in those days
you could fall asleep
& sleep an ancient sleep

old Communists—
they keep 'em alive with antifreeze—
populated dreams

they let you keep your nightmares
stalwart & stentorian
as your blowhard Uncle Death

nights were longer then
nausea and a red fever, sound

of typing in a far room
and the child who died
not spoken of

days broke in those days—

Later That Night

White, white light.
A man in a surgical mask
looms over him, frowning. Then dark. Hot

breeze over sand, Sahara
or the beach. His father's
pounding baritone.

They move him, not so
gently, to an ambulance, &
somewhere

beneath shock he feels
thumping of road slabs badly
joined, hears

an orderly joking with the driver—as if
he were cargo, which in truth
he is. A siren

growls. A two-way radio.
He is bleeding somewhere. Tries
to lift an arm

to wipe away the blood
pooling in his eyes—
or is that milk. The thin cry of his son.

Three Addresses
After Peter Davis

To an Ex

Are you sure you even
know me anymore?
Your line about

"drowning your feelings in booze"—
did you mean
sex, warm blue & numbing

as codeine? Or music,
the *Brandenburg* moment when
both flutes join the violin,

peaceful, erotic & sad?
Or did you mean
"steeping your feelings," &c.,

macerating them, like fingers
steeped in wine?

To Another Ex

Oh that stung, the line
about my taste in "lounge singers."
You meant—

Sinatra? Perry Como?
Fats Domino?
But you might

ask why
I was reading your
email in the first place.

To the Woman Who Met Me After the Concert

You ask how I was feeling.
I was stolen, entranced,
panicked, gutted

like a perch, pickled
like an onion, peeled
& left for dead—
a man drowning his feelings
in booze. Oh
it was exquisite.

Even Now

Eight minutes to go—the clock
is quiet   its tiny sprockets
synched to the stars. You hear

your own breathing   or hers   or
is that blood   throbbing

in the white hand that lies across the pillow?

Tonight I learned
the French for suits of cards.
*Le neuf de pique. La dame
de carreau.*

Eight minutes.
The heartbreaking small sound
of rain on outstretched leaves.

Even now   people are dying

The air is thick
with not knowing.   Her dream
makes her stir

a faint blue pulse of eye
under eyelid & you feel

her warm

outline across
the bed's dark inches

The Children's Castle

We're back together, you driving my new car
through November's first wet snow
to the children's castle on the high hill.

Something makes you think you
can take it onto the drawbridge,
over the moat, through
the oaken slab of a broken door, leaning
off its hinges.
                    I try to speak
but your gaze says no. The snow
has stopped, and in the gold
warm autumn far below us, couples lounge
in the old meadow.
                    Through
the door you take us, down a corridor
of mildewed carpet, past room
after room—abandoned but for dusty toys—
we float down many ramps & dank stone stairs

to the basement, from which
there's no way out, no-
where to drive.

A guard asks
what was she thinking. I think
how will this end

The Knife

We wake in the dark.
You ask what happened
and I ask *what were you doing with the knife.*
You reply *it was your dream.*

I ask what happened.
You reply *it doesn't matter.*
You repeat *it was your dream.*
Your hands on my back are cold.

Doesn't matter doesn't matter—
light in random patterns on the floor.
Your hands are cold,
the bedclothes damp,

random shadows on the wall—
down in the village, a noise like cats.
The night is damp.
I lie and study your eyes.

What were you doing with the knife.
I watch your eyes.
We lie in the dark.
You ask what happened.

Before You Go

I need to tell you what I
saw on the trail this morning
before dawn—a silent
darting in the shadowed litter
of last year's leaves.

It glided with me,
stopped, jumped ahead—
straight, low to the ground
like a tripwire.

I thought *groundbird, bat.* I thought
apparition.

It held a moment, quivering.

I thought *Stop for me.*
Stay & let me look at you.

Hello, David

Hello, David. Can I call you this morning?
David, are you sleeping later
& later, your air
perfumed with gin & Debussy? Are these pulp novels yours —
Dead Yellow Women, The Disenchanted, A Rage to Live

— or your mother's? Do you still take her
calls, or let them go to voicemail?
(Your front steps choked
with vegetation — chickweed,
jimsonweed, black medic, spurge.)
Hello, this is David. You know what to do.

David, is that you
in the ersatz Rockwell cover
of the *Saturday Evening Post*, 1958,
David, your china doll of a mother

shrinking from you, your chocolate hands
straining for the snowy folds

of her ball gown? David, did you know that
in the wilderness
of womanhood, men must keep

to the marked paths, while women

may move freely, David,

like birds, David, tree to tree?

Birthday Cards

On the first I compare him to a superhero. On the second
I express the hope we might speak someday.
The third, the one I send, has his camp picture. *Remember?*

It doesn't matter. The card comes back, addressee un-
known. Or did he return it himself? It bulges now
with added bulk. Coins perhaps

or skipping stones, except they're wet & leak something
like rust or dilute blood.

```
Three Nights
```

i. The Stranger

A bird flew into our tent.
You stirred in your sleep. I watched it
in the flat shadow of moonlight.

At dawn I opened the flap
to let the stranger out, but he was gone.

ii. After the Rain

The deer came. We heard them
through our sleep, chuffing
and pawing in that deerish way they have. Still

we slept, as we did
through the little earthquake
and the long war. But

in the egg-blue morning
you woke first
and called me to the window—the yard

strewn with antlers.

iii. Animal

Roused from a dream of arousal
by a screaming and scrabbling under the window,
I lurch barefoot into the yard and fall on the hairy thing,

wrap its haunches in my arms and
skid with it across the wet lawn, giddy—

Colorless

gray waves, white
houses &

clouds   his children
still in the water

with the ashes

from the gray
sack each

withdraws a handful
of him, mixes

him with river &
lets him drift

like thought

disperse
join

rise sink rise
& leave his slick

like smoke
on black smooth stones—

Water Music

She invites me to sleep with her and I say
why not. House out into the water—seawalls,
thick windows at wave height and a cracked ceiling
that lets in only so much winter light. And the singing,
endless singing.

Scissors

Size of a toddler, pea-green
& plush, legs
joined at the navel—human, only

with two heads. It
climbed the window last night,

green limbs knifing over & over
as its great eyes watched
helpless.

The Fall

Late-summer-afternoon Iowa haze:
lightning concusses the air.
A figure plunges to earth—
a telephone lineman, limp
as a shot bird.

       Dead on impact—
no, he springs to his feet
and looks all around him,
stunned but unhurt. My mother and I
watch through the living-room window.

She rushes to him and gives him a look
I've never seen.
          She doesn't ask
Are you all right. Asks,
Would you like a drink.

He looks unsurprised. Replies,
Yes I would.

Follows us inside. A tall man, all sharp angles.
A yellow hook—the one that failed him—
hangs from his belt. He watches

my mother. She offers another. They drink.
Such are the transactions of grown-ups.

Microfilm

your obit runs two full columns
ancient brittle type

like mica flecks
on March snow

tell me what you can tell me
in your own voice

so I know how it happened
& if you made it happen

without being told I know
if I turn the crank of this machine

you'll vanish forever
be strong you tell me

with a little bitter laugh
turn the page

head in the machine
hand on the crank

the snow on your back —

For Good

He wakes again & this time
it's for good. The bedclothes cold & damp,
a fever in the room. The upturned glass—
it's hard to breathe. He tries
to wake her & she won't—his hand
on the shallow hill of bones & hair
she was. Or was she even there.

Island's End

The road climbs to a bluff
      scrubby with sand & dwarf pine,
shocks of grass & bitter small flowers

high above another road (the road
      you were supposed to take)
you're late

so you double back &
feel time: a sweaty hand down
      your back

you think *Run*
& you think *Which way*
& *What's the point of running*

into a corridor — someone's house
stuffed chairs & copper pots on hooks,
      damp parlory smell of mourning —

impassive servants hold silver trays,
long spoons engraved
with the family C

Sorry so sorry — he was a <u>good</u> man

Your legs still slow, your tongue
        thick in your head. And here's
your father, not
dead after all but drunk

already at 10 in the morning — he lifts
his lidded face to you ...

Sleeping Through Irene

You dream of wading thigh-deep
on Main Street
lugging your oxygen—

dream of waking
to find water licking
at your thumbs

after the rain
you wake for real:

9 a.m. light
like hammered lead

sunken things
from upstate creeks
becalmed on pale water

& of course you think of the dead:
whales & coffins

& your own smooth self,
facedown in quiet water, waiting—

Greenwood

Layers of city, all the way down
to oyster beds & dredged

ashes subways tunnels escalators steam.

glary stones & dead names   black
mud, filling my dress shoes …

Gathered to Heaven 5-July-1891
& so on   wind stirs

the trees'   pale-green blossoms, heads
heavy with sex …

Aboveground I gaze past towers to the dark bones
of your plane, slipping

away   past two bright planets
& the new moon

Last Questions

Are you my brother or
a mockingbird?
Are you a cloud

or a flame in the high trees?
Breast—the woman's
or the stranger's—

in the moment or just before?

Teardrop, mountaintop
wind-shredded
flag of grief? Heavy stones

or drying blood?
Sunset or morphine,
fathom or pearl,

expanse of summer

or a frozen pond? Is that
a shadow on your forehead or

a gathering of sound,

like footsteps? The lawn—
does it descend

to the river or to nightfall?

January

Pines in the bright air, cedars, a busted oak—a sharp breeze
seizes snow in the meadow and swirls it into mist, and I think *fog of desire*

or a woman in a black peacoat alights from the bus on a 20-degree night and
looks as she crosses the street, plumes of breath rise, and I think *fog of desire*

desire in the fingertips, the toetips, the cold nipples—the background
drops out, tiny figures cross the frozen pond in noonlight, come closer—

I look into each face passing, and eye after eye warns me away.
Desire, desire, darkening the flesh, desire that can only come

to no good. I see your face in the fluorescent glare of our first meeting, try
to get my bearings in this mist, and have only the blank sky to tell me
which way is up.

Nighttown

The bedside clock is right for once: it's raining. Dark
& 52 degrees,

another month you look in a window & see someone
you thought you were but weren't—

imagine
a life alone, a different bedroom:

wet blowing in
through a window you forgot to close. To get up

in the thick fog
you'd have to think about the furniture,

linoleum, smells of ancients, magnolias
dropping meaty petals in the street.

Real Estate

Sell the house: you might as well:
you need a place

without so much light, steps
from downtown
(though the first step is a long one),

deathbirds in the dormers,
raptors of the genus Homo

nesting in doorways, kitchen
with embalming smells—
& on the rugs

ambiguous patterns,
north-facing windows like scrims.

Deer devouring roses, wind
roaming the porte-cochère,
flattening weeds,

& on the roof a fungus
of the genus Caligula:

it bursts into flame
and weeps
actual tears.

Room, Road, River, Rain

Tiled room, like a shower
or subway—sunlit

a girl you knew
not sure how well

you do what she wants

& something hurts is it
your legs, from all

the running, or your head
from trying to remember?

———

The room fades
& you're outdoors

the road is full of deer

their bodies spindly,
eyes incurious

you shut off the car
& let them surround you

———

How'd you get here?
teetering at the lip

of the edge of the cliff by the river

treetops too far
down to stop your fall

Sun far south,
over the bridge

clouds passing, passing,
passing

a bench, far down
where you could sit

silent in the sun

river making its soft
riverine hum

& eagles on the far side
shouldering the wind

———————

rain at night
smudge of a baseball diamond

light in the shallows
around home plate

an owl trembles
from a high branch

dark against dark

Cold

Benches filled with commuters. He
settles into one   beside me.

Of course I know his fate but how
could I tell him?   He makes small talk

of travel   of escaping his grown son.
Oh you'll escape all right   I think   cold

as a knife blade

Therapy

You hand me putty
to roll out—let my fingers
crawl it, parting strands of—
          what—
afterbirth, gluten, maidenhair—finding
buttons you've hidden

till one surfaces, hard
& shiny as an ache.

Last Night

A fluttering in the bedclothes:
he shows me something cupped
in his hands: a bird he's caught.
With a faint smile he
opens his hands.
It doesn't fly,
holds there, beating. He says
You can heal me.

To Ruth

You studied Italian
for this trip, pumping through
the phrasebook: *Mi scusi*
(for attention or apology), *permesso*
(when squeezing past someone).
The r's Midwestern. You'd sooner
shed your top at a nude beach
than roll an r. Then cancer,
as efficient as you were.

Fa bel tempo
in Chianti this morning, warm breeze
stirring the silvery olive leaves.
Last night we heard raspy breaths
under our window: a wild boar
snuffling in the moonlight.
You'd have laughed and translated:
Il cinghiale respira.

Here

Underneath all this—underneath the broken
branches, pale twigs, blown leaves, rotting
acorns, gray mud alive
with colonies of beetles, millipedes, spiderlings,
larvae in all their tiny shapes
and sizes, above the brittle sandstone crust
that holds all this up—is the accident's
imperceptible scour.

        That night, fifty years ago,
the car spun off the highway, pirouetting
(I imagine) gracefully, swaying and toppling
as it cleared the guardrail, scattering squirrels
and groundbirds, the door opening in midflight
and pitching him out, the belly of the roof
coming to rest on him.

        The night was cold.
Twigs and bits of snow dug into his bare neck.
And as rescuers strained to lift the car away,
he lay here (wishing he could help?) and saw
the last things he saw:

        Blue-black sky.
Pinpoint stars. Night pines.
Tall oaks.

Some of these poems first appeared in the following journals:

Adirondack Review, Barrow Street, and *Podium.*

David Corcoran was born in New York City in 1947 and was raised in nearby Rockland County. A lifelong journalist, he began his career as a boy, covering sports at the local paper. He attended Amherst College and continued in newspapers, ultimately working as a writer and editor at *The New York Times,* where he retired as editor of the weekly section, *Science Times.* His poems have appeared in *The Adirondack Review, Barrow Street, Fovea* and *Podium.* David Corcoran died in 2019. This is his first book.

Publication of this book was made possible by grants and donations. We are also grateful to those individuals who participated in our 2021 Build a Book Program. They are:

Anonymous (16), Maggie Anderson, Susan Kay Anderson, Kristina Andersson, Kate Angus, Kathy Aponick, Sarah Audsley, Jean Ball, Sally Ball, Clayre Benzadón, Greg Blaine, Laurel Blossom, Adam Bohannon, Betsy Bonner, Lee Briccetti, Joan Bright, Jane Martha Brox, Susan Buttenwieser, Anthony Cappo, Carla and Steven Carlson, Paul and Brandy Carlson, Renee Carlson, Alice Christian, Karen Rhodes Clarke, Mari Coates, Jane Cooper, Ellen Cosgrove, Peter Coyote, Robin Davidson, Kwame Dawes, Michael Anna de Armas, Brian Komei Dempster, Renko and Stuart Dempster, Matthew DeNichilo, Rosalynde Vas Dias, Kent Dixon, Patrick Donnelly, Lynn Emanuel, Blas Falconer, Elliot Figman, Jennifer Franklin, Helen Fremont and Donna Thagard, Gabriel Fried, John Gallaher, Reginald Gibbons, Jason Gifford, Jean and Jay Glassman, Dorothy Tapper Goldman, Sarah Gorham and Jeffrey Skinner, Lauri Grossman, Julia Guez, Sarah Gund, Naomi Guttman and Jonathan Mead, Kimiko Hahn, Mary Stewart Hammond, Beth Harrison, Jeffrey Harrison, Melanie S. Hatter, Tom Healy and Fred Hochberg, K.T. Herr, Karen Hildebrand, Joel Hinman, Deming Holleran, Lillian Howan, Thomas and Autumn Howard, Catherine Hoyser, Elizabeth Jackson, Jessica Jacobs and Nickole Brown, Christopher Johanson, Jen Just, Maeve Kinkead, Alexandra Knox, Lindsay and John Landes, Suzanne Langlois, Laura Lauth, Sydney Lea, David Lee and Jamila Trindle, Rodney Terich Leonard, Jen Levitt, Howard Levy, Owen Lewis, Matthew Lippman, Jennifer Litt, Karen Llagas, Sara London and Dean Albarelli, Clarissa Long, James Longenbach, Cynthia Lowen, Ralph and Mary Ann Lowen, Ricardo Maldonado, Myra Malkin, Jacquelyn Malone, Carrie Mar, Kathleen McCoy, Ellen McCulloch-Lovell, Lupe Mendez, David Miller, Josephine Miller, Nicki Moore, Guna Mundheim, Matthew Murphy and Maura Rockcastle, Michael and Nancy Murphy, Myra Natter, Jay Baron Nicorvo, Ashley Nissler, Kimberly Nunes, Rebecca and Daniel Okrent, Robert Oldshue and Nina Calabresi, Kathleen Ossip, Judith Pacht, Cathy McArthur Palermo, Marcia and Chris Pelletiere, Sam Perkins, Susan Peters and Morgan Driscoll, Patrick Phillips, Robert Pinsky, Megan Pinto, Connie Post, Kyle Potvin,

Grace Prasad, Kevin Prufer, Alicia Jo Rabins, Anna Duke Reach, Victoria Redel, Martha Rhodes, Paula Rhodes, Louise Riemer, Sarah Santner, Amy Schiffman, Peter and Jill Schireson, Roni and Richard Schotter, James and Nancy Shalek, Soraya Shalforoosh, Peggy Shinner, Anita Soos, Donna Spruijt-Metz, Ann F. Stanford, Arlene Stang, Page Hill Starzinger, Marina Stuart, Yerra Sugarman, Marjorie and Lew Tesser, Eleanor Thomas, Tom Thompson and Miranda Field, James Tjoa, Ellen Bryant Voigt, Connie Voisine, Moira Walsh, Ellen Dore Watson, Calvin Wei, John Wender, Eleanor Wilner, Mary Wolf, and Pamela and Kelly Yenser.